Dealing with A Narcissist

The Beginners Guide to Recovery

Table of Contents

Introduction 1

Chapter 1: What is a Narcissist 2

Chapter 2: Narcissistic Personality Disorder 5

Chapter 3: Faces of Narcissism and Gaslighting 12

Chapter 4: Major Types and Subtypes 22

Chapter 5: How Do You Know When You're Dealing with a Narcissist? 27

Chapter 6: Dealing with the Mind Games 34

Chapter 7: Having a Relationship with Narcissists 43

Chapter 8: Step One—Acceptance 56

Chapter 9: Step Two—Becoming Aware and Increasing Your Awareness 59

Chapter 10: Step Three—Detach with Love 66

Chapter 11: Step Four—Building Your Self Esteem 69

Chapter 12: Step Five—Change Your Reactions 72

Chapter 13: Step Six—Being Assertive 74

Conclusion 77

Introduction

Thank you for taking the time to purchase this book

This book covers how one can deal with a narcissist and will teach you the initial steps to recovery.

You will learn what narcissism is and differentiate it from modern notions of this term. You will learn its effects on the person suffering from narcissistic personality disorder and how it affects the victims of narcissists.

The book also covers how to deal with narcissists, their mind games, the setting boundaries, accepting realities, build your self-esteem, how to detach with love, how to be assertive, find nurturing and growth, and other helpful insights.

This is not an all-encompassing book but it is enough to walk you through the initial steps to recovery and freedom from narcissistic abuse.

Once again, thanks for purchasing this book, I hope you find it to be helpful!

Chapter 1:
What is a Narcissist

Nowadays the term "narcissist" is used as a blanket term for anyone who seems to be obsessed with getting admiration or sparking interest to themselves. Although these two are definitely characteristics of a person with narcissistic personality disorder, it doesn't necessarily mean that you're a narcissist if you have them.

You see everyone craves for some attention from time to time. And of course, who doesn't want to be admired by others too, right? There are times that you actually need these two aspects of social life in order to get some much needed boost to your self-esteem.

Be Careful About Throwing Labels Around

However, just as one expert on the subject has pointed out, sometimes we carelessly label people as narcissists even if they really are not. Sometimes the person we think is a narcissist is just a bit overly too egotistical to say the least.

Nevertheless, there are real narcissists.

And on top of that there are a lot of folks out there who have suffered because of them.

A lot of times it's the loved one who is a narcissist. It can be a father or a mother—many times it's the father who is a narcissist; and some studies suggest that there are more narcissistic men than women. However, there are times when it's the mother who is the narcissist and she has a huge impact on her daughter.

The worst kinds of narcissist are the malignant narcissists. We'll go over the different kinds of narcissists in a separate chapter of this book.

The majority of the victims of these outrageously self-centered people are often left so devastated and debilitated by their personal experience with their narcissistic family members. These victims often develop post-traumatic stress disorder.

Real Narcissists and NPD

When we downplay the word narcissist to include everyone who has a penchant for being overly self-absorbed we are actually downplaying something that we sometimes fail to notice. We are watering down and trivializing the pain and suffering that is experienced by actual people who are victimized by real narcissist.

In this book, when we mention the term narcissist as applied to someone we are actually referring to someone who is diagnosed with narcissistic personality disorder and not the everyday term we sometimes use to describe people with an over bloated ego.

That means someone posting tons of selfies on social media doesn't count. Someone who speaks too loud whenever they're on their phone isn't exactly one. Your sister who hogs the bathroom mirror and stays there for hours isn't a narcissist.

However, someone who compulsively and repetitively lies to his girlfriend and insults her to get an ego boost is probably one. Someone who psychologically manipulates others to manage and control them may be one.

Note that there are many narcissists among us and not all of them are malignant. Sometimes we too need a healthy dose of it (i.e. self-attention, praise, and feeling the spotlight at least from time to time) in order to help us get through the big stressful events in life.

Dr. Susan Whitbourne, professor emerita at the University of Massachusetts Amherst, says that it may be hard to believe but there are narcissists who are actually loving and caring human beings.

They are functional and contributing members of society and it isn't right to throw them in the same category as narcissists who are absolutely malignant and abusive. These productive and healthy narcissists belong to the category of autonomous narcissists. We'll cover the different types of narcissists in a later section of this book.

Just note for now that there is an entire spectrum when we refer to narcissists. And in this book we will usually refer to narcissist as someone who is diagnosed with NPD or narcissistic personality disorder. Some may use the term as a mere pejorative but that isn't really fair or accurate.

Chapter 2:
Narcissistic Personality Disorder

It should already be common knowledge nowadays that the term "narcissist" comes from the Greek legend of Narcissus. As the legend goes, the young Narcissus fell in love with his own reflection in the water in a nearby lake.

The Legend of Narcissus

And thus we can see the fixation on oneself as one of the characteristics of this disorder. Another thing detail from the legend that we can bring to the forefront here is that of Echo, the nymph who actually fell in love with Narcissus.

Narcissus couldn't love her in return even though Echo was so attracted to the young man. All she could do in the end is to repeat back what the youth said to her. Eventually she is reduced to an echo without any voice of her own and only a manifestation of the man she adored.

This is also characteristic of the relationships between narcissists (aka people with NPD) and the people who are related to them—especially the children. They are left with no identity of their own and to the narcissist their only purpose is "echo" back to the narcissist who controls them.

Narcissistic Personality Disorder

Narcissistic personality disorder or NPD for short is actually one of many other kinds of personality disorders. It will be pretty steep before you can say someone has it. As it was pointed out in the previous chapter, not everyone who has a narcissistic tendency has NPD.

Someone with NPD has a characteristically inflated sense of what they perceive to be their own self-importance. It is grandiose and usually out of proportion or out of touch with reality. They are more than just guys or girls who feel entitled to everything—they will even demand and command it and will feel deprived or wronged if they do not get that preferential attention that they hunger for.

Other than this deep and excessive need for admiration as well as attention from others, they also lack empathy for others. Thus things always result in troubled relationship for them. Sometimes they have trouble understanding why other people just won't appreciate them.

However, there is a dark and deep secret that everyone should know about people who are diagnosed with NPD. It is that they too are vulnerable. The tough, lying, manipulating, and mental controlling person on the exterior is nothing more than a defensive layer for a fragile self-esteem that gets crushed under the weight of the slightest critique from another person.

Someone with NPD usually faces a lot of relationship problems. But their behavior and habits also cause trouble in the other facets of their lives. They get in trouble with their financial affairs, at school, work and work relationships, and of course they also raise issues in their personal affairs and relationships even within their own family.

When they do not get the admiration and attention that they feel they deserve, they get disappointed and unhappy. In an instant, the crowd in that party has become a lot less interesting. The relationship that he is having with his girlfriend has become unfulfilling—and thus a lot of narcissistic guys go from one relationship to another.

Narcissistic Personality Disorder: Signs and Symptoms

Note that the severity of the signs and symptoms of NPD will be different from one patient to the other. Yes, we'll call them patients since they technically have personality or mental health issues.

These people may display or manifest any of the following symptoms if they have NPD:

- A sense of self-importance that is exaggerated and is out of touch with reality
- They require constant admiration
- They expect that they will be treated as someone who is superior even if there is no evidence to support that claim or view.
- They have a high sense of entitlement
- They also tend to exaggerate any achievements they have had in this life.
- They are often preoccupied with grandiose fantasies about themselves
- They exaggerate their actual talents (sometimes they don't have any such talents)
- They believe that they should only associate with people who are equally special as they are—as a result they belittle others who they perceive to be of a lesser status.
- These people are often so obsessed with their looks and their status in the eyes of others.

- These people have a tendency to monopolize conversations
- They also expect unquestioning compliance
- These people often take advantage of others so that they can get the things they want
- People with NPD expect to be given special favors
- They are either unwilling or unable to recognize the feelings and needs of other people
- They also believe that other people are envious of them
- Usually they behave arrogantly
- They often envy others
- These people will usually insist on getting the best of everything because they feel that they deserve it or are entitled to it.

How a Narcissistic Person Reacts to Negative Treatment or Criticism

- Secretly they feel humiliated, vulnerable, insecure, and ashamed
- They become moody
- They get depressed
- They feel a difficulty adapting to change
- Major problems dealing with the stress
- Problems regulating their own behavior
- They experience emotional problems
- They lash out in rage
- They start belittling other people to regain that superior status they believed they lost
- They feel slighted even with the smallest or insignificant remarks

- They also begin to have interpersonal problems especially with that person whom they think is criticizing them

Causes of Narcissistic Personality Disorder

The actual causes of narcissistic personality disorder are currently unknown. Note that the development of a personality is a very complex process. The same can be said of personality and other kinds of mental health disorders.

The possible causes may be linked to the factors that help to shape one's personality, which includes the following:

- Genetics
- Environment
- Neurobiology

Complications and Risk Factors

There are more men with NPD than women – that means this disorder is more common for men. Nevertheless we can say that the men who have it were not born with it. It has been observed that the onset of NPD begins during the teenage years and also as a young man enters early adulthood.

Of course, young children may show some signs or inclinations towards narcissism but having such signs won't mean that the child will develop NPD later in life. The seemingly huge fixation on themselves is nothing more than a part of their growing years and a natural part of life. That means all of us actually have such traits when we were younger.

It is also believed that parenting styles that are either too overprotective or on the opposite end of the spectrum those that are neglectful can contribute immensely to the development of NPD. There are also hints that genetics and neurobiology may have an impact on the onset of this disorder.

It has also been observed that people with NPD may also develop other conditions as well even though they are not directly related to the occurrence of this disorder. For instance, some narcissists may engender suicidal thoughts and related behaviors.

Some people that have been diagnosed with NPD may also have a history of alcohol dependency or even illegal drug misuse. A lot of people that have this condition are also at risk for developing physical health problems.

There are also those who have to deal with anxiety and depression. To think that they can cause anxiety and depression in others it is interesting they too are also subject to these emotional problems as well.

Again, as stated earlier, people who have been diagnosed with NPD have trouble maintaining healthy and productive relationships. That is why a lot of them have problems in school and later in their professional lives as well.

Can It Be Prevented?

There is no known way to prevent the onset of narcissistic personality disorder. Well, that is simply because we do not know what causes this disorder. Nevertheless, there are ways in which the condition can be properly managed.

Here are a few ideas:

- Parents who have narcissistic inclinations can attend parenting classes
- They can also solicit help from social workers and therapists.
- People with NPD can also participate in family counseling and therapy.
- With the help of experts and trained professionals, they can learn ways to cope with emotional distress.
- They can also learn how to communicate well with others
- It has also been observed that with early detection and treatment they can properly manage this and other types of mental health problems.

Chapter 3: Faces of Narcissism and Gaslighting

NPD is one diagnosis that can be made for a person with a mental disorder. However, when all things are considered, there are actually three faces of narcissism. There are several ways to classify people with narcissistic personality disorder. One way to make these distinctions is to base it on how they treat other people.

Some experts suggest that you can actually build rapport with narcissists if you know the specific type or class that they can be classified. However, there are also experts who say that you should stay away from them as much as possible. Note that there are dangerous classes of narcissists that you should stay away from.

The Three Faces of Narcissism

With that in mind we can categorize narcissists by the way they treat others. In order to make the right categorization, we need to ascertain certain characteristic traits—there are 9 of them to be exact.

As stated earlier, the three most characteristic traits of a serial narcissist are grandiosity, an excessive need for admiration, and a complete lack of empathy. However, there are other behaviors that people with NPD will exhibit.

They will also have any of the following habits or behaviors:

- Speaking ill of friends (even close friends) and partners
- Discarding people who they deem are already useless
- Gaslighting

Note that not all narcissists will exhibit the same set of behaviors. We have mentioned an extensive list of behaviors in chapter 2 of this book. A narcissist doesn't need to have or display any of the said behaviors on those lists. If someone you know regularly displays at least 5 of the behaviors in that list then you have a clue that they may be a narcissist.

Exhibitionist vs. Closet Narcissist

According to one expert you can classify narcissists according to their upbringing or according to the way they were raised by their caregiver. Some become closest narcissists while others become exhibitionist narcissists.

Exhibitionist Narcissism

Exhibitionists are the most common face of narcissism. To be more politically correct, it is the most common manifestation of this disorder. Some people refer to it as the grandiose narcissist or grandiose subtype.

Just like little children, narcissists that belong to this category crave for a lot of attention. They have no ability to empathize with the feelings of their guardian when they were little and so they cannot empathize with other people as well when they have grown up.

They cannot understand or they are unwilling to understand how others feel when they are affected by their actions and personalities. It is also unfortunate that there are some parents who unwittingly encourage narcissistic behavior when treating their children.

For example, some children have been brought up thinking that they belong to an elite family. They are made to believe that everyone in the family is superior to other people. Some family members are highly intelligent, very skillful, and highly talented. They are made to believe these things even though it is far from the truth.

These kids grow up in a home where there is an overabundance of excessive praise and over indulgence. Exhibitionist narcissists believe that they are amazing, smarter, and better looking than other kids.

It is also interesting that they rarely feel that they are insecure. When they brag about how great they are they also put down other kids at the same time. They always have someone to compare themselves to.

You can recognize them quite easily because they are usually rude to other people. And at times they may even be cruel to people serving them. One key attribute that you can observe is that they carelessly ignore the reactions of other people. It's like they don't really care if they hurt other people's feelings.

Closet Narcissism

You can say that the closet narcissist is the complete opposite of exhibitionist narcissists. Now even though they are not as showy in their attempts to belittle, malign, and manipulate people, closet narcissists are still narcissists. They just manifest their narcissism a lot differently.

Some people call closet narcissists as vulnerable narcissists. Some of these folks may have grown up with another narcissist in the family. For instance, it is possible for a narcissistic daughter to grow up with a narcissistic mother.

That daughter may have competed with her mother several times as she grew up. However, she may have found that her efforts are futile so she has chosen to do things behind the scenes instead.

Closet narcissists are characteristically introverted. Yes, it might be hard to believe but there are introverts who are also narcissists. Sometimes they may feel conflicted since part of them want to express how special they think they are but they still prefer to remain alone and distant from society.

But don't make any mistake; these people will take any form of entitlement when they can. They may not act out all haughty as exhibitionist narcissists but they will have that sense of entitlement covertly.

For instance they may tell stories about this great guy or girl they know. They will tell what special qualities that person may have. But in reality that special individual that they are practically bragging about is no one else but themselves.

Closet narcissists do have persistent self-doubts, believe it or not. They usually look for someone with whom they can attach to. Usually that is someone who they see as their ideal self. They exhibit passive aggressive behaviors in order to get attention and also solicit a reaction.

Here's an example. A mother that goes by the name of Juliet (not her real name) is a single mom who lives with her daughter Annabel. Juliet has been diagnosed with vulnerable narcissism and has been identified as a closet narcissist.

It has been observed that Juliet has a tendency to demean her daughter Annabel especially when there are other people around. The effect of course is that the mother and daughter get estranged even though they live under the same roof.

Annabel seldom pays any attention to her mother Juliet. You can say that she has grown tired of her. To solicit the attention that Juliet craves primarily from her daughter to who she has formed an attachment to, she would at times attempt suicide.

However, before committing such acts (or at least attempting them) she would make sure that her daughter will see and witness everything. One time she held a knife to her wrist. But before attempting to even cut her wrists, she called out to her daughter Annabel.

Of course the daughter reacted—she would save her mother time and again. Of course all these stunts are deliberate and there is an ulterior motive behind each one of these suicide attempts.

When Juliet sees that her daughter Annabel starts showing empathy she will start the blame game and guilt tripping. Juliet will pin the blame on her daughter Annabel saying that she was about to commit suicide because of her.

Of course the mother and daughter duo also get into fights. Annabel will sometimes have enough of the demeaning behavior and words from her mother. However, Juliet somehow finds a way to spin things around so that the blame all goes to her daughter.

Some experts say that closet narcissists are more devious and therefore are more dangerous compared to exhibitionist narcissists. That is because you never know how and where their attacks will be coming from. At least with exhibitionist narcissists, you have it all laid out under the sun.

The covert nature of the efforts of a closet narcissist makes them more difficult to deal with. They gaslight their victims so much that they don't know they have been manipulated to the core.

Gaslighting: Warning Signs

Gaslighting is one of the common tactics used by narcissists. Gaslighting is also used by dictators and cult leaders as well. They are especially used by introverted narcissists or closet narcissists. However, do take note that narcissists can make people feel gaslighted whether they are done covertly or openly.

Gaslighting is an effective tactic—more than we think it is. A narcissist gains power when their intended victims start to question their reality. Note that anyone is susceptible to gaslighting.

It is performed slowly and the targets don't know how far they have been manipulated until they have been brainwashed to a huge degree. Using this technique, a narcissistic husband for instance may have already manipulated her wife so much that she feels like she is already losing her mind.

The following are some of the techniques used by narcissists to gaslight their targets and victims:

1. **Telling Blatant Lies**

They have the ability to tell lies with a straight face. Yes it is an outright lie but sometimes if you investigate what they say sometimes it checks out as true. And then you are left to wonder what things they say are real and which ones are false.

They tell lies as a precedent. There is a motive behind the lies. Some lies are partially true to convince you that they are not lying. Some lies are small and they are a setup for a bigger lie that they will tell later on. Everything's a setup.

2. **They Use People and Things That Are Dear To You**

They have done their background research on you before they gaslight you. They know if you value family and they will know how much you cherish your kids. They will use the things that are important to you when they attack you. It is all in an effort to disarm you so that they can manipulate you.

3. **What They Say Doesn't Match Their Actions**

A narcissist will be on talk but little on deeds. The words they blurt out in public is just for show and they are meant for something else. Don't pay attention to the big words they use, pay attention to their actions. That is where the truth of their intentions lie. That is at the heart of the issue.

4. **They Will Use Confusion to Weaken the Other Fellow**

They want you to feel confused because they know that when you are confused you are vulnerable. You will be open to suggestions when you don't know what to do next. They will try to uproot normalcy and stability in your life.

When you are already confused they know that you will naturally look for someone who can give you guidance. The narcissist will then place himself or herself strategically as that person. When that happens you are already ensnared.

5. People Misalignment and Isolation

A narcissist will be on the lookout for someone who will stand by them with them. Let's say a narcissistic mother has established that attachment to her daughter. Once that attachment has been made, they will say bad things about the people the daughter associates with. She practically ruins the reputation of other people in the eyes of her daughter.

The goal is to malign others so that the mother can isolate the daughter. The daughter will not know who to trust anymore. Thus she returns to her mother since she is the only one she believes will be there for her through thick or thin. Isolation therefore becomes a tool to control the victim.

6. They Tell You That Everyone Else is a Liar

A narcissist will want you to believe that the best source of information is no one else but he himself. They will manipulate their victim's belief system. They will make their targets believe that other sources are flawed or perhaps are just plain lying.

They will make you believe that the other members of your family are liars or just don't know what they are talking about. They will also manipulate the other person's views that the popular media is a lie or is at least misguided and full of misinformation.

And then they will again position themselves as the most credible source of info. A narcissistic best friend will use this tactic to make his close buddies believe no one else but himself. If they want to know about any guy in school then he's the go to guy.

Believing that lie will make you question everything. The only source of reliable info that you will know is the narcissist who is actually gaslighting you.

7. Denial

To confuse you further, when you discover some inconsistency in the narcissist's statement they will deny having said or done anything. They will even have the tenacity to deny it even if you present proof. They will find a way to twist and deny factual information. The goal of course is to keep you in the dark and confused.

8. The Gradual Breakdown

The narcissist will slowly and gradually break you over the course of time. They will lie every now and then. Manipulate you little by little. Feed you false information one small bit at a time. Over time things start ramping up. This is the experience of a little child going through the motions of gaslighting—their young minds being shaped into believing lies.

9. A Little Bit of Kindness and Positive Reinforcement

Does dad really hate me or is it something that I did that made him angry? At one point the narcissist is hurting you, shouting at you, and even hitting you. However, there were golden moments when he would just be very loving.

This confuses people especially the victims of narcissists. One day they will be praising you but the next day they will hate you like you're the worst person on earth. Every move is calculated to confuse you and to keep you away from your defensive edge. That way you won't come to a point where you will completely turn your back to the narcissist.

10. They Project Their Deeds onto You

A narcissistic husband may accuse his wife of cheating. However, if you do a little digging you will discover that he was the one cheating on his wife. Every evil deed whether it is true or not is placed on your lap.

The idea is to put you on the defensive. It is a lot more tiring to defend your position from any kind of accusation. The narcissist will shift the burden of proof to you so that you will get exhausted—too tired to notice the actual misdeeds carried out by the narcissist.

Chapter 4:
Major Types and Subtypes

Experts have classified narcissists into 8 types. Three major types and the rest are subtypes. The three major types of narcissists are the following:

1. Classic
2. Vulnerable
3. Malignant

We have covered the classic and vulnerable types of narcissists in the previous chapter so we will only touch on them slightly here. We will cover the malignant and other subtypes of narcissists.

Classic Narcissists

Classic narcissists are also known as the exhibitionist type of narcissist. They are the sort that always wants to attract attention. They enjoy being in the limelight and they want to be the life of the party.

As it was described in the previous chapter, these people are boastful, they want to attract attention, and they brag about their accomplishments. On top of that they also expect that others will flatter them with attention and admiration. They also expect special treatment from others even though it isn't warranted or even if they don't deserve it.

They also believe that they are superior to other people. Those are the reasons why these narcissists are also known as grandiose, high functioning, and exhibitionist.

Vulnerable Narcissists

Again, this type of narcissist was already covered in the previous chapter so we'll only describe them slightly here. Narcissists that belong to this type or class are also known as closet narcissists, fragile narcissists, and compensatory narcissists.

These other names are rather descriptive of them. These are the ones that wouldn't want to have the spotlight focused on them. In fact some of them don't like to be the center of attention.

They work covertly and manipulate other people from the sidelines. Believe it or not some of the narcissists who belong to this class are rather generous. They are perceived as being kind to others but do not want to take on central leadership roles.

They are happy to serve as assistants or maybe as workers. However there is always a motive to everything they do. Their generosity will be noticed from time to time and so they get a morale boost from time to time.

Because of their good nature they will also attract people. Some of these people they attract they can target. Because they have been generous and kind, the people they have done service to will feel somewhat under a debt of gratitude.

It's like silently making people owe them and they will definitely collect one day. Even though they do not sound or look like it, they definitely feel superior to other people.

Malignant Narcissists

Malignant narcissists are also known by a more menacing name—toxic narcissists. That says a lot about them. This is the type of narcissist that has no other goal than to dominate another person.

This type of narcissist is highly manipulative and they are equipped and willing to exploit other people. They will resort to deceit in order to get what they want. If that doesn't work then they will resort to aggression and violence.

Many narcissists that belong to this category are antisocial. That maybe the biggest trait that makes this type unique compared to the first two. Some experts compare malignant narcissists to psychopaths and sociopaths.

Note that they also do not have any remorse for the things that they have done. Some of them also have sadistic streaks. You may even say that they enjoy seeing others suffering because of the things that they have done. Toxic narcissists can be covert narcissists (meaning they do their thing under the radar—more of that in a little bit) but they can also switch to being exhibitionists as well. They can switch to either methodology quite easily as needed.

Narcissist Subtypes

There are five narcissist subtypes other than the three major types mentioned earlier. The five subtypes include overt, covert, somatic, cerebral, and inverted narcissists. Note that the major types of narcissists can go into one or more of these subtypes.

1. **Overt Narcissists Subtype**

Overt narcissists are showy and they're easy to spot. They will be quite visible in their efforts to control and manipulate other people. They openly take advantage of people, which makes them noticeable. The overt narcissist is what everyone usually thinks a narcissist is like. Classic narcissists and Malignant narcissists can fall into this subtype.

2. **Covert Narcissists Subtype**

The covert narcissist is the opposite of the overt narcissist. They work their way to manipulate and control other people secretively and stealthily. They may apply passive aggressive methods as they see fit. Their victims may not know that they were already being manipulated until everything has been said and done. Vulnerable and Malignant narcissists can be placed in this subcategory.

3. **Somatic Narcissists Subtype**

Somatic narcissists are those that are obsessed with their appearance. They may also be obsessed with their youth. You can find them in gyms, sports clubs, and also in the fashion and beauty scene.

This is the type of narcissist that will not want to be outshined by others – especially their partners. They will usually hang out with other people who are less attractive than they are. All of the three major types can belong to this subtype.

4. **Cerebral Narcissists Subtype**

Cerebral narcissists are not exactly obsessed with their good looks. They are more interested in being more knowledgeable than others. You can tell who they are the moment you start a conversation with them.

They are the know-it-all types and they will compete with you when it comes to knowing better in every subject. The goal for these people is to make everyone in the room impressed with how much they know.

Instead of focusing on good looks, their main tool to get the advantage over other people is their wit and knowledge. They will use it to gain the upper hand. Note that any of the three major classes of narcissists can belong to this subtype.

5. Inverted Narcissists

Inverted narcissist is the subtype where you would place narcissists who remain subservient to other narcissists. They are vulnerable and covert at the same time. Some people call them "victim narcissists" because they seem to be happy with being number two to another narcissist who is already dominating. Some have speculated that narcissists who belong to this subtype are grew up and survived having been deserted by their parents.

Chapter 5:
How Do You Know When You're Dealing with a Narcissist?

So how do you know if you're living with or are dealing with someone with NPD? Of course to truly diagnose someone that will require some professional help. However, there are telltale signs that might help you confirm your suspicions.

Again, all of us are guilty of having narcissistic leanings from time to time. But remember, the big difference is that it never becomes habitual. A person with NPD will habitually display the behaviors described below.

On top of that they will be largely unaware of the effects of their actions on the people around. Well, it's either they are unaware or are just unconcerned. Here are some of those signs that give them away:

#1—They Hoard and Hijack any Conversation

Narcissists love to talk about themselves and they just can't help it but jump on the opportunity to steal the conversation. Don't hope to get a two-way conversation. That's not happening.

Your narcissist friend may be sitting there as if listening or paying attention, but he's just waiting for his chance to butt in and talk about himself. It's always a struggle to get your feelings and thoughts pushed into the conversation.

At some point the discussion will be like him saying "okay that's enough about me, what about you?" You will think that you will now have your chance to have your say on the matter but you have to understand what your narcissist is actually asking you.

He's not asking you for your opinion about the matter. He's asking you for our opinion about him. It's not about the case in point but it's about him and possibly his relationship to the point of the discussion.

Well, you might have a chance to put a word in. However, if what you have to say is not anything about the narcissist, your words and thoughts will be dismissed, maybe corrected, or will just largely be ignored.

#2—They'll Be Happy to Interrupt Your Discussion

This habit is just as annoying and is rather related to the first one mentioned and discussed above. A person with a malignant narcissistic tendency can't help himself but interrupt any conversation.

It's a poor social and communication skill but they do it anyway. If they hear a conversation that is at least slightly interesting they will be more than happy to butt in and join the conversation.

However, they're not there to contribute or challenge the ideas that are being discussed. Oh well, they might throw in their two cents on the matter but that's not the goal. After butting in and interrupt the flow of thoughts already being displayed they will shift the course of the discussion back to themselves.

And that is the main point for them. If it's not about them then it's not worth talking about. What's the only thing that is worth talking about? The topic should be about them and beside that there is nothing else that should be any more interesting.

#3—They Violate Boundaries

People with NDP have no respect for personal boundaries. They do not respect personal space, possessions, feelings, thoughts, and others. They have wanton disregard for these things.

They habitually overstep these boundaries and are totally inconsiderate. For instance, narcissistic parents will barge into their children's rooms, rummage through their things, and everything else as if they were their own. There is no sense of privacy for them.

They repeatedly break obligations and promises. They borrow money and fail to return them. On top of that they show very little remorse for their actions and pins the blame on their victims.

#4—They Break Rules Habitually

You can say that the malignant narcissist enjoys being able to get away with breaking the rules. They also feel some form of satisfaction from breaking social norms. For instance, some narcissists will habitually give less than the normal tip for services rendered while other narcissists will over tip in an effort to show off.

Some prefer to break multiple appointments. Others take pleasure in being able to steal office supplies. Some narcissists on the other hand enjoy breaking traffic rules.

#5—A False Sense of Entitlement

Now, this is a biggie for tagging an actual narcissist. They have a false sense of entitlement. They feel that they are deserving of preferential treatment. They believe that people should cater to their needs—and cater you must rather instantaneously as if you were in the presence of royalty at that.

This rather bold assumption is aggravated by the fact that they often feel that they can do so without having to be considerate in return. You can also say that in their point of view, the world revolves around them. They should be the center of your world.

#6—They Project a False Grandstanding Image

A person with NPD does a lot of grandstanding. They do this in order to impress others and of course to make themselves look good. Some have called this the trophy complex. They try to project a false image of themselves religiously, socially, sexually, romantically, physically, culturally, academically, professionally, materially, and/or financially.

These so called accomplishments are substituted for what they are really inside. They will look good in the eyes of the public to cover up their real selves. A lot of this grandstanding is actually exaggerated. This is done in order to get other people's love, acceptance, and admiration.

#7—A Grandiose Personality

One telling sign that you're dealing with a narcissist when you observe a grand aggrandizement in their personality. They will see themselves as some kind of really important person in the lives of the people around them.

They will believe this so much about themselves. Their exaggerated view of their own personal importance can go so far as they will believe that other people won't make it on their own without their very important contributions. It's the "without me they are nothing" sort of thinking.

#8—He is a Charmer

In spite of the egotistical air about them it might be hard to believe that there are narcissists who may have quite a charming personality. These people are rather persuasive and even charismatic.

Some of them are even great leaders in the office, the marketplace, or other professional field of endeavor. Once they have their sights on you they can be pretty charming. That is why some chronic narcissists can make women/men fall head over heels for them.

At first they will make you feel special and really wanted. However, certain patterns have been observed. These people will tend to get bored and lose interest in you after they have gotten what they want.

They can drop people without any second thoughts. They won't care if you get hurt when they break up with you. You will be left thinking what you have done wrong. They were sociable, engaging, and caring at the beginning.

However, as soon as you no longer fulfill their desires, these malignant narcissists will no longer give you their all just for your attention. They would have moved on to their next subject of interest and you were just a fancy footnote on their long list of love affairs.

#9—They are Very Manipulative

They manipulate people to use them as extensions of themselves. This can happen to people who have family members who are narcissists and it can also happen to friends and in other social situations.

A malignant narcissist may provide for a son or daughter very well sending them to the best schools and giving them the best things in life. However, there is a purpose behind all that. Again, the purpose is very selfish.

For example, a daughter who is raised by a narcissistic mother will be dressed up and look really pretty. This is called a dolling up of the child. The praise and admiration that the child gets for being pretty and polite is seen as a reflection of the greatness of the mother.

In the work setting, a boss who is very narcissistic can take credit for the accomplishments of the entire team. At the other end of the spectrum, the narcissist can also manipulate others so that they can cover up any possible flaws or adequacies. Again, everything is all self-serving and the narcissist will manipulate people just to get what they want.

A narcissist has a variety of tools to manipulate others. They actually play a lot of mind games on people. For instance, they may use guilt to manipulate their children making them feel like ingrates pointing out all the sacrifices that the narcissistic parents have done for their children. We'll cover this and other manipulative tools and tactics that narcissists use in a separate chapter.

#10—They Arouse Negative Emotions in People

You can tell if you are dealing with a narcissist if he or she can incite negative emotions in you. They make you feel insecure and maybe a bit off balance. They do this in order to put other people down and put themselves in the limelight.

They may throw a fit or even a tantrum if you disagree with them. They perceive slights where there is not and they make you feel awful about yourself.

They will be very quick to ridicule others. Notice how fast they criticize and blame other people's faults. Again this is an effort to make other people around them feel inferior. A lot of narcissists, and this goes without saying, are emotionally abusive. Again their goal is to boost their egos.

Chapter 6:
Dealing with the Mind Games

Someone once compared malignant narcissists as great con artists. You know what, that guy might be on to something. You can say that these people have become masters of the art after years of practice.

They have learned to use a variety of tactics just to get what they want. They can also hide who they really are and you wouldn't notice that you were dealing with a narcissist even after many years of associating with them.

Experts cite three manipulative characteristics of people who have NPD:

1. They are serially numbed to the possible suffering that they have caused in others.
2. They're very good at analyzing the personalities of other people and they can spot a suitable target on sight.
3. They are also very good at hiding any kind of violent tendencies that they may actually have.

If you can spot these traits or at least catch hints of them then you will be saving yourself from a lot of pain and suffering because of their manipulative techniques. Now, having said that, it should be pointed out that spotting a manipulative person is difficult.

Narcissist Mind Games

To find them out, you need to know what you need to look for. The good news is that we can categorize the tactics that narcissists use. We have them listed below.

1. *They Dig Into Your Life's Details*

Surprisingly a lot of manipulative people, narcissists included, would love to hear your story. Some might talk about themselves a bit but they will first want to hear your side of the story.

It's a ploy to find out who they are dealing with. They will feign interest in you and inquire about your life's details. They will poke into your plans as well as into your thoughts.

They need to know how to best manipulate you. In other words, the information you so endearingly give away will be used against you. A narcissist is not interested about you per se. He will want find out your weaknesses and where they can pitch themselves in.

The good news is that if you suspect someone trying to pry where they don't have to, you can always counter politely by spinning the discussion around. Stop talking about you and ask more of the other guy.

Check out his or her reaction. Is there any direct eye contact when you're being asked? Is there any invasion of personal space? A narcissist may fall for it and start his braggadocio. Well, he likes to be the life of the party anyway, right?

2. *The Subtle Show of Superiority*

Someone who is out to manipulate others won't be that bashful about proving how great they are. Your narcissist will talk about facts, figures, and numbers about themselves. A lot of the things that he will puff out are things you can't even pronounce.

After finding out about you they will talk about things that you are not familiar with. Makes sense right? Why give you a chance to butt in and control a subject under discussion?

Now even though you may know the subject that they are talking about, narcissists won't let you budge in with your ideas. They will water down anything that you would have to say. They may dismiss it as trivial and shift the discussion to some other subject where they can show off their better qualities.

The goal behind it all is to show how much better they are with the added intent of establishing their influence over others. They put themselves up on a proverbial pedestal so that they can be in a position of control.

One way to dismantle this tactic is by asking the narcissist about his source. He may point out a fact that may be backed by medical studies. If he does that then challenge his position by asking for his sources.

Ask for proof and you can also ask them to elaborate on the subject.

Oh wait, did he just use an uncommon word—something that you just heard right now? Ask him to define his terms. Even if they do know the meaning of the word you will notice something change in their behavior.

They basically don't want to be interrupted.

Interrupt them in their barrage of statements and you will see that the emphatic person a while ago has left the room. In his place is a know it all who is disinterested in what others have to say. He will not be actively listening to you but is just waiting for his chance to butt in and pound you with more info.

How do you catch a fish? That's one way to unmask this mind game for what it really is.

3. *Overwhelming People with Negativity*

Another mind game that narcissists like to play is to overwhelm people with negativity. They will speak ill of people and display some of the worst manners that you can ever see.

Some bully type narcissists will maltreat people around them. Some talk down on people while others may even resort to violence. This is a tool that they use to back people off and manipulate others directly.

Part of the goal is to instill fear into others. They know and understand that fear is a powerful tool. Aggression is also another tool at their disposal which they will use to complete this tactic.

They will make you feel inferior and negative. They will humiliate you. And then they might do something totally different, like talk to you as if they care about you. All of that will make definitely confuse you. In the end they will make you feel that you can't do anything without them. The goal is to subdue you before you become a problem for them.

It will be very hard to cope with this kind of mental and emotional tactic because a lot of times your emotions will be way too charged to respond. This is especially true if you are closely related to the narcissist like a spouse, a parent, or a sibling.

Nevertheless, your cue is in the big and immediate change in behavior. Your father becomes so very negative all of the sudden. Your boyfriend suddenly blames you for everything, becoming oh so very upset all of the sudden.

For some reason your brother becomes really aggressive. You were having a good time and then all of the sudden he would make a scene right in front of other people.

Sometimes the negativity is constant. They always treat you differently compared to your brothers and sisters. A narcissistic boss would compare your best effort and results to that of his or some other employee that he favors.

Other than identifying these patterns you can also test the other fellow by trying to remain calm. In a later section of this book, we'll go over a few things that you can do in such situations.

You can also counter by thinking that the negativity that they're throwing at you is a joke. Act as if it was something funny and see if the narcissist tries to attack you again with the same tactic. If they do that and also attack your jokes as well then you know that they are trying to manipulate you using negativity.

It will take some effort to ignore the humiliation and insults that will be thrown your way. Being able to remain calm and unaffected in spite of the barrage of negative words and sentiment is a huge statement to the narcissist that you are not someone who will be controlled.

4. Acting Innocent

Another tactic that malignant narcissists will employ is acting innocent. They may do this if they want to pin the blame on you and other related situations. Something wrong happens and they will act as if they are unaware of the incident.

Even though it is really their fault they will never sound and look guilty. If they are accused they will have a pretty logical excuse to throw at you. If you that it was their fault they can play the role of the victim in the situation.

If you doubt and your guts are telling you that there's something wrong then let it go for now but keep investigating. Ask the narcissist more clarifying questions next time especially after gathering more evidence.

If you have ascertained without a doubt that the narcissist is truly guilty then you can confront them dead on—unless of course you're dealing with a violent person then you should get help instead but keep the evidence.

They Feed on The insist

5. Insecurity of Other People

Malignant narcissists are very good at detecting people with insecurities. In fact some of them even actively search for people like that. They will even find a way to get some sort of connection to that insecure individual.

Being with insecure people will elevate their emotional state. It will give their morale and their sense of superiority a big boost. If that person has found some kind of a backbone they will use it as some kind of a target so they know how high and just how superior they have to be.

The insecurities of others are used to mask their own insecurities. They will act like someone who stands out amongst a group of people with issues. That way they can assert themselves. It's as if they feed on the emotional charge that the people give to them. These people need someone to hang on to and look up to and they will be there to supply just that.

It's also funny that when they know your specific issues that they may bring it up in public. They may start to talk about it even if there are other people who may hear you talking.

One tactic that you can use is to deny or lie about an alleged insecurity even if it is true. Don't give the narcissist something that he can use against you. Now, see how the narcissist will react.

Notice that sometimes a narcissist will flare up and their energy levels will go up when you try to escape from a trap they set. Regular people would just dismiss whatever it was but a narcissist won't let it go.

The long term solution is of course to face your insecurities so that a narcissist won't have anything to pin on you. Face whatever you have to deal with and don't let yourself remain a victim.

6. They Tend to Twist the Facts

Can malignant narcissists get caught? Yes they can but they can also wriggle a way out of a sticky situation. Narcissists can weave a web of lies that can leave people confused about what is real and what is not.

They can twist the facts to make you doubt your own memories. They can set you up so that you will only see what they want you to see. They can also spin stories so that even though they were caught they will appear as the victims. They sort of shift the blame on someone else or at least reduce the fault that they are to shoulder.

It will take a lot of effort to unweave the lies. You should gather the facts; verify the names, the places, and events that the narcissist will mention. If they mention someone that you can contact then look them up and ask them about their version of the story.

7. They Use Emotional Pressure

Another mind trick they use on people is emotional pressure. They put you under pressure until you burst. Well, you will get an emotional outburst to be more precise. They will play a game of stress and relief.

After your emotional outburst (after you've had enough of all the stress you had to put up with), surprisingly your narcissist will be there to console you. They will even act as if they are really sorry. They may even appear to want to make amends.

At that point a lot of people get emotionally disarmed. When that happens they can better control that person. That individual has lost the ability to make sound decisions.

Be careful when someone uses this technique on you. It is also hard to discern and you need to be truly vigilant. Notice the hallmarks of this mental game. Ask yourself the following questions:

- Who was it that caused you stress and pushed your buttons?
- Who is it now that is giving you comfort and relief?
- Why is it that the one that caused you stress and the person that is now giving you emotional release is one and the same person?
- Why is that singular person telling you what to do next?

Don't be afraid to ask that person why he or she pushed you to the limit. If that person who triggered your stress avoids this discussion then stop all interaction and create distance. You know that that person is manipulating you.

Chapter 7:
Having a Relationship with Narcissists

Sometimes there is just no way of getting around it but to have and maintain that relationship with a narcissist. This is true of people who have narcissistic members in their family.

There are cases where the narcissistic tendency of the brother, sister, or parent is workable. That means the narcissist isn't absolutely abusive and you may be able to assert your position in the family.

It all depends on several factors. Your age, your emotional state, the type of narcissism manifested by your friend or family member, and several other factors become part of the equation.

Are Narcissists Capable of Falling in Love?

Now this is part of the equation really. If you want to have a relationship with a narcissist you should know if that narcissist is truly capable of loving you. Well, the first question is if a narcissist is capable of falling in love—that's good place to start.

And the answer to that question is yes.

Believe it or not, there are narcissists who are capable of falling in love.

Narcissists are human too so yes they are capable of falling in love. The next question that you need to answer is critical. Coz it is one thing to be capable of falling in love and another thing to be able to reciprocate love.

So, are narcissists capable of reciprocating your love?

The answer to that question is rather complicated. You can say that it is a yes and also a no. There are a lot of factors coming into play and that complicates everything.

For one thing, a narcissist may show affection but on a different level and also on a different degree. Remember that their personality can suck the stability that you have in your system.

Their ego boosting behavior will come into play and there will be times when those behaviors will interfere with the narcissist's ability to fully express his or her love. They are very insecure creatures whether they would like to admit it or not.

Those insecurities of theirs combined with your emotional entanglements and insecurities will not always make a lot of well-mixed chemistry. In fact, you should brace yourself for a lot of conflict. Expect a love-hate relationship that is full of turmoil. In fact narcissists may not even be aware that they are already covering up for their insecurities.

Understand What Is Required

If you decide to establish and/or maintain a relationship with a narcissist you should know that there will be a lot required of you. A huge amount of your time will be needed and your presence will be demanded.

Yes, narcissists can express their love for you but they will also require you to reciprocate that love or to at least express it profoundly in return. You see, you will have to assure narcissists in order to appease their anxieties.

There will be times when it will be like you need to give unconditional love. Well, sometimes that is exactly what a narcissist will want from you.

Some narcissists fear abandonment and they will do everything—and I do mean everything—to keep you with them. Well, that is if they have grown to love you. But remember that there will be many days when it will be like they are pushing you away.

They will be angry at you, they will put you down, and even insult you. Sometimes it will feel like the narcissist is pushing you away. But then again you'll be dragged back into loving arms.

Remember that they will be driven by this seemingly illogical need for approval. Because of that they will do things that will seem to sabotage your relationship. It's a cycle really—a crazy cycle of love and hate.

Nevertheless, there is no harm in trying to love a narcissist even if the one you're trying to love has severe symptoms of NPD. There will be people who will not understand why you're putting up with all the bad treatment.

Some would even say that your narcissist doesn't deserve you. And that is part of the package—there will be pressure within the relationship and there will be pressure from without.

Just remember that the bottom line here is that you chose to be in this relationship not them. It's a gamble and you can't play it without being fully into it.

What You Have to Put Up With

Expect the following behaviors from your narcissist. Note that the items on this list were written down by an actual *female narcissist* who was in a relationship. Think of them as being part of a confession. At least now you get to see things from their point of view:

- You think that you need me but I actually need you more.
- I'm actually very curious about you.
- I try to be better—God I tried!
- When I try and try really hard it really means something.
- I can be quite creative.
- I would love to feel you even for a fleeting moment
- I definitely would love to make you be at your best—especially if you being at your best makes me look good too.
- And yes, I do look good both outside and within.
- I like you to look good.
- I can be daring too.
- One of the things that I fear the most is when you find me out.
- When I see your weaknesses I sometimes think I have won but it also means that I have failed in some way and that is why I am angry.
- I'll have to admit that vanity is a peculiarity with me.
- I always keep my mark—that would be you.

- I feel that I am overused.
- Yes, I admit that I am damaged.
- But I will always need your approval and I might force it out of you sometimes.
- I'm afraid that one day I will become boring to you.
- I have wants—a lot of it—and sometimes nothing can fill that craving.

Setting Boundaries

If you are to maintain a relationship with a person diagnosed with NPD or someone you know to be a narcissist, then you need to set boundaries. These boundaries will help establish some structure especially when you are dealing with someone closely related to you like a parent, a lover, or even your boss or supervisor.

The boundaries you set will protect you from being manipulated by your narcissist. Boundaries also establish safeguards from threats, physical, as well as emotional abuse. You can consider them as a safe haven or a safe zone whenever you interact with narcissists and other abusive people.

You will have to be assertive when you set these boundaries. Note that abusive people, including narcissists, will try and resist the boundaries that you may have set. They will dismiss it as something trivial or whimsical. But you have to stand by them and assert them until the narcissist realizes that you are serious.

They need to know that you won't budge and they can't talk you out of it. They need to understand that it's either you will have these boundaries or else you're out of their lives.

Stages of Boundary Setting with Narcissists

There are several stages that you need to go through in order to set boundaries with narcissists. You need to be clear and specific with every point and rule that you make. You also need to be sure about your demands before you communicate them.

Remember that a narcissist will challenge you on every point, which is why you should be very specific about what it is that you want. Every boundary you set should be clear and explicit.

Expect to state your boundaries repeatedly and you should be consistent about your expectations. You should also state each point calmly – don't show the narcissist that he or she is getting to your nerves.

Well, you don't need to be elaborate with each point but you should always be crystal clear about what you want. Just stick to the facts even though you haven't gone over all the itty gritty details.

Here are the stages of boundary setting:

1. *Drawing the Line*

You wouldn't want to set boundaries with a narcissist unless you know what they are capable of. That means you have had enough experience with him or her to know enough and exactly where to draw the line in your relationship.

When you draw the line you should also come to terms with certain behaviors that you will be willing to accept. You should also communicate which behaviors you deem unacceptable.

When you communicate your expectations you don't have to provide a detailed narration. You don't need to provide details explanations why you want these boundaries set or why this specific boundary is needed.

In other words, when you draw the line keep it short, quick, and decisive. You don't need to explain yourself to the narcissist.

Keep in mind that as you are doing your spiel (yes you can write everything down and just read it to him), the narcissist will try to intimidate you, stall you, put you on a guilt trip, and use other tactics to derail you

2. *Prepare an Exit Plan*

Notice that even though you have set boundaries and even though you have repeated them time and again that your narcissist friend or family member will still ignore them or even challenge them from time to time.

There will be times when the interaction will become too toxic for you. Every time things become too unhealthy or too hurtful then you should have an exit plan for every situation.

When such a thing happens, remind the narcissist about the boundaries that you have set, and then execute your exit plan. Get out of there quickly.

There is no need to ask for permission since that will only give the narcissist a foot hold. There is no need to explain or provide the real reason why you have to exit the conversation.

You can give an excuse like you have an appointment or even pretend that you have a call (you'll need to have your phone on hand). Or you can just say you have to go and act like you're in a hurry—no explanations needed.

3. *Prepare a Clear Agenda*

Earlier we mentioned that you need to draw the line and clearly identify certain boundaries in your interactions with a narcissist. I would suggest that you write each detail down.

Why?

As stated earlier, your narcissist will challenge each point or even try to find loopholes in your propositions. Or sometimes he or she will just try to aggravate you and make you lose your temper.

You can choose to answer or have prepared answers for certain queries. For instance, you may set a boundary about not calling you when you're at work. Your narcissist may ask why and you can give a one sentence answer for that—there is a rule in the office to limit phone calls while you're clocked in.

That should be enough. Any further inquiries as to why should never be entertained. You have already given your reasons and you shouldn't have to explain your point further.

What if the narcissist pushes on and keeps on asking anyway?

You don't have to stay on topic. The narcissist keeps on prodding, then you should shift to the next topic or boundary you want to set. You can ignore further queries.

4. There is No Need to Elaborate and Justify Your Position

Remember that you don't deserve to be at the receiving end of all that questioning. You don't even need to elaborate on things.

Now, here's an important rule of thumb—never divulge information that is personal.

If you give that away then you are giving the narcissist an opening that he or she could pry into. They may keep that in mind for a long time and bring it out or state it for a fact next time.

5. Point Out What the Narcissist is Doing

After you have set the boundaries you want—remember that you can make adjustments as needed. You should be able to point out or call out exactly what the narcissist is doing.

Let's say the narcissist starts insulting you for a perceived failure on your part.

You can call it out by saying "you're insulting me."

Just mention it. And then pause.

If the narcissist ignores you or just prattles on, say it again. "You're insulting me."

And then pause. Wait for him/her to realize what you're doing. Say it with conviction and say it as if you have caught the thief red handed.

It could be anything that the narcissist is doing to manipulate you: insult you, lie to you, putting you down, etc.

After calling out what the narcissist is doing, you should mention the boundary or rule that you have set and then apply the consequence (which is the next part of the equation).

6. *Set and Apply Consequences*

Every rule and boundary that you have set should have a corresponding consequence when the narcissist breaks it. Remember that a narcissist will be prone to ignore or even violate a rule that you have set.

Consequences should also be clear and you should have set them ahead of time. You don't want to make up the consequences as they come. Remember that a narcissist will figure it out and challenge your rule if you keep changing the consequences. Rules are rules and the consequences are part of the rules.

You don't want your rules and boundaries to lose their credibility because you were inconsistent with this important part of law or rule formulation. The goal again is to not give the narcissist a leg to stand on.

7. *Custom Tailor the Rules and Consequences*

Since you already know enough about the narcissist then you should customize the rules and boundaries accordingly. You know what ticks them off then you should create rules and boundaries about that.

You know that they will tend to put you down when it comes to academic achievement, then set boundaries with regard to that part of your interaction. You know that they can pretend to be in an emergency when you're away then you can make arrangements and also set boundaries whenever you have to leave the house.

You should also keep your rules and boundaries within proper perspective. Your boundaries are there for your protection but not to harm or get back at the narcissist in your house. The rules are there to provide structure so that your interactions with each other will remain healthy.

Remember that the narcissist in your life will naturally be toxic all in an effort to hide his or her own flaws. They have insecurities too and it may be hard to admit but they only behave in the most unruly ways just to create a façade of their own anxieties and fears.

Make sure that the rules and boundaries that you have set will benefit you as well as the narcissist as well. In the long run, having these boundaries will help teach your narcissist how far he can go with his interactions. They are teaching moments and it may take a lot of time before they realize that.

On your part, you have to be patient and apply these boundaries consistently. And yes a lot of times it will be like being the adult in the relationship all falls on your shoulders.

8. Keep the Focus on You and Your Children/Spouse

Sure the boundaries and rules that you have set should be fair and humane. But remember to keep your focus on yourself, your children, and your spouse if you are living with a narcissist.

The children need the most protection of course. That means the majority of the boundaries and rules should be on them. The children won't understand why grandma or grandpa is so mean to them or why they can be mean one time and then oh so kind all of the sudden.

Note that if narcissist is already negatively impacting your kids, you should keep them away immediately. Move to a different house with your kids if you have to. If you find the slightest hint of abuse of any form (verbal, physical, emotional, etc.) then contact child protection services immediately.

The narcissist in your home will still be a narcissist. In fact they may be narcissists for life and there is no way that you can change them. All you have to do is to accept this fact. We'll cover this in greater detail later.

9. *Be Compassionate to Yourself*

You have lived through a lot of abuse from the narcissist in your life. Sure the boundaries that you have set may help them change their ways but that is just a bonus. The primary objective of the rules and boundaries that you have set are for your benefit.

Allow plenty of time out moments.

Even if it seems that the interactions are healthy if you feel at any time that you need some time out from your relationship with the narcissist in your life then take it. You don't have to suffer for them because you have already suffered enough.

Remember that you are not impenetrable like a rock. You have feelings and toxic relationships can take a toll on you. Another frustrating thing is that you have to set the boundaries over and over again.

At times it would be like you're always starting from scratch. Adjust your expectations and create more opportunities to protect and nourish yourself.

In the next chapter we will go through the actual eight step process to dealing with narcissists in your life.

Chapter 8:
Step One—Acceptance

This is the first step in the 8 step process to dealing with a narcissist in your life. In the previous chapter we have gone over the steps on how to set boundaries with them. In this eight step process you will learn the next steps in order to care for yourself and your family while you have a relationship with a narcissist.

These steps will be helpful to children who grew up being raised by narcissists. They will also benefit men and women who have narcissistic spouses. They can also benefit you if you have other family members who are narcissists. They're family and you just can't get rid of them, which is why you need to know how to cope with and live with them.

Acceptance the First Step

Since you can't run away from that narcissist in your life—maybe it's your spouse, your best friend, your parents, or maybe a sibling—your next logical course of action is to accept the fact that you do have to deal with it.

You can limit your interactions. That is all well and good. However, you should also plan for those small moments when you have to interact with them. You should also create contingency plans in case they also interact with your children or your husband or wife.

If it is your spouse that is a narcissist you should have contingency plans and ways to explain to your kids why you have to separate.

You have to come to terms with the difficult fact that the narcissists won't be able to reciprocate the good things that you have done for them. You will be misunderstood at times and people around you might misunderstand you as well -- and sometimes that is more painful.

Recognize What's Really Going On

Awareness and acceptance is the hard and tough road that everyone in a relationship with a narcissist must tread on. It's a tough one simply because it is hard to believe that your relationship was a lie.

After all, how can a mother not love her child? How can a husband go on blaming his wife for everything? How can a wife be so critical and demeaning to her husband? Believing those things as opposed to accepting that they are not just phases that these people are going through is such a hard choice.

That is why someone who is in a relationship with a narcissist should first become fully aware of what's going on and accept it for what it is. Sometimes you just have to accept the fact that the narcissist in your life didn't really love you at all.

Do some introspection. Ask yourself—is the behavior of your narcissist husband the same or in any way similar to that of your parents? Do you feel like you are attracted to people who have that strange sense of entitlement?

Are you easily compelled to follow the lead of such a person? Note that it is very easy for sensitive people to feel compelled by narcissists. However, note how it eventually feels inside with that person.

You don't feel good about yourself, right? If you end up not feeling great about yourself, feeling like you're praising him more than uplifting yourself then there must be something wrong.

Trust your feelings.

If your spouse is a narcissist and the relationship is choking the life out of you then get out of that relationship fast. If the narcissist in your life is your parents then establish those boundaries. Create a safe space for yourself. Find help and join a support group.

Remember that narcissists will never think that they are wrong. They will always put the blame on you. They will always think that you are the problem. In the end you'll just feel like a doormat.

Acceptance is the more difficult path but it is your first step to freedom.

Acceptance also means that you start believing that you deserve more than what your narcissist is giving to you right now. It is the first step to truly loving yourself.

Chapter 9:
Step Two—Becoming Aware and Increasing Your Awareness

The next step is to become more self-aware. One of the effects of being in a narcissistic relationship is that you lose your sense of identity. This is especially true of children who grow up with a narcissistic parent.

They lose a sense of their identity. It will be as if they only serve their purpose in the eyes of the narcissist in the family.

Remember that the crafting of one's identity and personality starts from childhood. Your personality is your own concoction taking bits and pieces from the world around you and reacting towards them in your own way.

You lose all of that when you are raised by a narcissist. In a sense, they become your life. You do what they want you to do. You act as they want you to act. You lose your sense of self in the process and you become nothing more than a reflection or a manifestation as it were of the narcissist in your life.

A lot of people who have survived narcissistic abuse don't realize that they have been robbed of their self-identities until they have left that relationship they had with a narcissist. It takes a while before that reality kicks in. When it does, they rarely know what to do because what they are and what they want has been taken away from them.

6 Signs That a Narcissist Has Robbed You of Your Sense of Self

It may be difficult to realize that you have been robbed of your sense of the inner child. You've been preyed on and you were forced to live in such a way as to serve the purposes of a narcissist.

Healing from identity loss is a definitely a long road. However, the first step to it all is to realize that you were a victim. Here are six signs that you can use to gauge that fact.

1. *You missed out on a lot of childhood opportunities*

Healthy relationships are the kind where both parties support each other. In the case of a parent and child relationship, there are many firsts in the child's life where the presence and support of a parent will be a big help.

Do you remember a time when your mother or father came to school for your recital, soccer game, etc.? Did your narcissistic parent/spouse/friend attend your graduation, the party for your promotion, and other exciting and life changing moments?

If not then you have one sign. There wasn't much in the way of support in your relationship, was there?

2. *Your life doesn't seem to move forward anymore*

How have you spent the last few months (or years?) of your life? Have you been doing all you just so you can please your mother/father/brother/spouse/best friend? Does it feel like you've finally hit a plateau in your life? Nothing you do pleases or wins the approval of that narcissist, right?

Of course nothing does.

And nothing ever will.

Your best option at this point is define what you really want to do with your life and then do it.

3. *You don't think you're attractive enough*

Do you feel uncomfortable in your own skin when you're around the narcissist in your life? Of course you don't. They will always say that you are too fat, too ugly, your legs are too long, your hair is never right, and you get all that negative vibe even after all you can do.

They criticize your appearance and even your abilities to put you down. Why? It's all about control.

4. *You're always a failure in their eyes*

This is sort of linked to point number 3 above. A narcissist always puts you down. Some children have grown up to be straight A students and some even graduate at the top of their class. But still their narcissistic parent still thinks that they're failures.

You make salesman of the year. You're constantly the employee of the month. You're the best manager in the company. But you always fail in the eyes of your narcissistic father.

5. *They're stuck in your head*

Is every decision you have to make based on what your narcissistic parent/spouse/friend says? Are they always in your head? Does it always end up like "what would he/she say?" If that is the case, then you have already given up the power to choose for yourself.

6. *You have no idea what to do now that you are on your own.*

The victim of a narcissist ends up as having no other purpose in life but to be a part of that narcissistic relationship. Take away the narcissist from the equation and the victim loses a sense of purpose.

They don't know what to do next. They don't have a life purpose. They don't have a sense of meaning or sense of mission. Some have used unhealthy coping tools like drugs and alcohol.

How to Regain Your Own Identity

Now that you have broken free of the narcissist's hold, so, what's next? That is the lonely and scary question for a lot of victims of narcissistic people. They need to find their own self—mage and they need to get some inner healing.

You can't always point the way for them. And the scary part is that they must learn to find their own life paths on their own when they have lost the skills to find the said path.

With that in mind, here are a few suggestions that have been found to help people who are on this peculiar crossroads in life.

- *Find and surround yourself with people who support you*

These victims need help—a lot of it. Sometimes the first people who you should be talking to are the very people the narcissist told you to push out of your life. Did you grow up with a narcissistic mother? Did she tell you that your father was evil and that he wasn't enough for you? Then try to connect with your father and see how that turns out.

You can also find support groups on line. There are plenty of raised by narcissist parents and surviving narcissist groups on the internet. You get to learn about other people's experiences and you can also share your own.

Learn from other people's road to recovery. See if you can find tips and other ways to cope with the situation from others. Share to them what you have found and what works for you. It will be a great help to know that you are not alone in this type of experience. Others have found their road to freedom and you can find yours too.

- *Do something that your narcissist told you that you aren't good at*

Consider this as a way to validate the truth—that you could do it all along. It could be a hobby, a career, anything. However, make sure that this is something that you once wanted to do but were prevented from doing so. Let it be something that the narcissist prevented you from doing for the longest time.

- *Take everything slowly*

Making new changes in your life can be overwhelming. This is a new stage in your life – a new found freedom as it were. Sometimes you will find it hard to communicate with other people. For the first time in your life you are deciding something for yourself.

No one's there to tell you what to do and no one is telling you what you can or can't do. Take everything one step at a time. All of this is part of the huge healing process that you will have to go through.

If you were prevented from making new friends then start slowly. Find acquaintances in first in your neighborhood. Try something that you haven't done before—but do one thing at a time. Try to find things that interest you.

Don't rush. If you rush things you might find yourself using toxic copic tools and that will not get you moving forward in life.

- *Set your boundaries*

If you have moved away from your narcissist friend/family member don't be surprised if they try to reconnect with you one time or another. That is why we have covered setting boundaries in the previous chapter. You will need them from time to time if you have decided to leave your narcissist and forge your new life.

However, if you are stuck and you can't get away – maybe it's your mother or father who is the narcissist, then you still have some sort of connection even though how little it may now be; you will still have to deal with that relationship.

But if you have set these boundaries then you have some form of order on how you should interact. You have drawn the lines and the narcissist in your family must abide by those rules or you're out. It's the way you protect yourself from that toxicity and continue in your path to healing.

- *Block and/or cut them out*

At some point, enough is enough. There are times when you just have to block and cut the narcissist out of your life. This is especially true of abusive relationships. If you need to get a court order to keep the narcissist out of your hair then do it.

Note that sometimes keeping away from the narcissist's presence will feel uncomfortable. Some people have gotten so used to the feeling of being dominated that they feel that there is something missing without it.

It will take a while before that feeling goes away. Trust me, I've been there.

Sometimes it's scary. But if you follow the tips and steps mentioned above, you will move on with your life. It's never easy but the rewards will be worth it.

Chapter 10:
Step Three—Detach with Love

Detaching with love is a term that has been used by experts to mean that you are cutting off a person in a relationship minus the resentment. You are letting go not because you hated that person—yes you can let go of a narcissist without hating them.

And detaching with love gives you a chance for closure—at least on your side of the bargain. The narcissist may not be willing to let go or even forgive. But you're doing it anyway not because you no longer want to care but because it is no longer your business.

Detaching with love will be something like this:

> *Someone calls at the office asking for the sales department and he's asking about a delayed delivery. But you're in the B2B division. You understand that this person you're talking to is a customer, which means he is valuable to your company.*
>
> *What do you do? You politely tell him that he called the wrong number. You then inform him which division of the company you're in, apologize for the misunderstanding, and then transfer the customer to the right department.*
>
> *You didn't take ownership of the customer's problems. But at least you cared enough to point them in the right direction.*

In the case of a narcissistic relationship, you detach from your narcissist not because you don't want them anymore in your life. You don't deal or even touch whatever drama, comment, or whatever they hurl at you. But you point them elsewhere—to therapy maybe.

Whatever the narcissist has to say or do, it's no longer your business. Why? It is because now you have to take care of your life. If you have children now then your business is to care for the children and not what the narcissist is trying to do to you.

It's a new start. That's your business.

Back to Acceptance

The first step to detaching with love is to accept and realize that there is nothing at this point that you can do to help your narcissist. There is no longer any way you can fix mom.

Remember that it should have been mom (or dad, or whoever your narcissist was) who should have been taking care of you and not the other way around.

It is time to accept the fact that you can't help your narcissist no matter how hard you try. And now it is time to let go. There is no need for you to step in, it is time for the narcissist to take responsibility for his or her actions.

That way they are learning to do something for themselves and you are now on your way to recovery and healing. It's the perfect win/win for both of you.

Chapter 11:
Step Four—Building Your Self Esteem

Building your self-esteem after narcissistic abuse is so much different from other situations. When you find yourself out of luck and lost your job and you hit rock bottom, you can find yourself getting up. No problem, right?

Why is that?

Well, your self-esteem is intact. You may have lost everything but you still have a lot going for you. You may have lost your job but you still have your skills, your connections, and your innate ability to rise to the occasion.

You are equipped with all the tools.

Starting with Nada

Building everything from scratch after a narcissistic relationship isn't like building anything from scratch. No it isn't.

To be more precise, it is like building something out of nothing.

You have nothing to begin with after narcissistic abuse. The very coping skills that you can fall back on aren't there because the narcissist robbed you of that very thing.

Even the ability to believe in yourself is none existent in this kind of reality.

And that is what makes it hard.

How Do You Build Your Self Esteem?

The situation is not helpless. And it all begins with you. Start by picturing out what shapes your beliefs. Start with what you had wanted all along but were hindered from doing so. You need to identify what you really want and along the way build your self-confidence.

Here are a few suggestions that might help you:

1. Start with small and simple things

You don't have to start big. Do the little things first especially the things that your narcissist told you that you could never do right. That may include the following:

- Taking care of how you look. Go to the salon. Get a makeover. Look beautiful.
- Fix your car, get it detailed. If you're into motorcycles then get your bike fixed. If you're into art or music then start with those talents. Learn the rudiments and work things out slowly.
- Decorate. Get the house plumbing fixed.
- Get a job. Any job. Anything that will make you feel independent is great.

2. Realign your internal dialogue

Notice that your inner voice sounds like the narcissist, right? Your inner dialogue is just as negative. It's time to fix it. Find affirmations and read them and repeat them to yourself in front of a mirror every morning. You can take a 2 minute affirmations break whenever you need it.

There are affirmations apps that you can use. These apps can play the affirmative statements about you and all you have to do is to take 2 minutes of your time to listen to them.

3. Volunteer to help others

One of the things that you can do is to help others a lot less fortunate that yourself. Volunteer for a soup kitchen or some other charity. You will find that in the act of uplifting another you are also healing your own soul.

4. Set small goals

Choose a small goal—it could be anything. It can be something like moving into a new apartment, landing your first job, earning a certain amount of savings, paying off a small debt, or even traveling or going on your very first road trip.

You can even make a bucket list out of your small goals. One day you will look back at your list and notice all the things that you have achieved—all the things that your narcissist told you that you can never do without them.

5. Stop comparing yourself with others—realize that there are people who want to see you succeed.

You have always been compared to the narcissist when you were still in that relationship. Now that you are done with it, stop comparing yourself to others. Find other people who are willing to support you. Find those who will be happy for you when you achieve something new.

Chapter 12:
Step Five—Change Your Reactions

In judo there is a saying that if you want to beat your opponent (well, the goal in that sport is to be able to throw your opponent, that's how you win), the first thing you need to do is to get a reaction.

For instance, if you want to throw a person forward you first need to pull him backward. You can't keep using your own force to throw or beat the guy. That's just not energy efficient. You will exhaust yourself eventually that way.

The way to do it is to pull the guy first so that he will pull against you. Now that he is going backward as he pulls against you, you will follow through with the direction of the energy. Execute a throwing technique that goes in the direction in which he is going.

That way you use his energy against him. The bottom line is that you win without a lot of energy expenditure.

You can also use this emotional judo with a narcissist.

Emotional and Psychological Judo

Grab your journal and try to recall every encounter you had with the narcissist in your life. Write down or make a journal entry of every detail you remember.

Pay attention to a few important details:

1. What did you do that triggered the interaction?
2. What was the narcissist's response to your action?

3. How did you react to the narcissist's action?
4. How did that empower the narcissist to manipulate you?

For instance, you messed up dinner—well, maybe you cooked a wonderful dinner (which could be the case) and the narcissist could never cook it the way you did. That was your number 1. Number 2 is that your narcissist mom (or whoever it was) insulted your cooking. Maybe she said that it was good but you could never had done it without her teaching or coaching.

What's your number 3? Maybe you cried, you kept quiet, or you apologize. Record your response. And then try to recall how the narcissist responded to your reaction.

Now, next time that happens, change your reaction. Check out the response. You will find in these experimentations that if you change your response you can gain the upper hand and control the situation instead of being controlled.

You are now aware of what the narcissist is doing and you can control which way the interaction will go.

You have control.

Chapter 13:
Step Six—Being Assertive

Being assertive is a habit. It is not being hostile. The narcissist you were with wasn't assertive. He was abusive. Being assertive means knowing what you want and knowing how to voice them out with confidence.

As you might have already guessed, you won't get to step 6 without working your way to the first 5 steps mentioned in the previous chapters. Those are prerequisites before you can come up with this 6th step.

Formulate those habits mentioned earlier first and then come back to this step after you've done all of that.

7 Habits of Assertiveness

The following are small actions that you can turn into habits. These habits will eventually help you build your own assertiveness. Somewhere along the way these habits will help you build your assertiveness.

1. *Learn more about assertiveness*

Find assertive people. See what they do. Find out how they act. Understand their points of view. If they authored a book or if they write blogs then subscribe to their works. Let their insights fill you. If you can find a way to interact with them, then do so. Attend symposiums, if it's someone at work then talk to him or her. Let their assertiveness rub off on you as it were.

2. *Keep your communication in line.*

You don't want to talk like your narcissist. Remember step one above. Find your role models and follow their communication styles. Practice.

3. *Speak simply and directly*

If you're the stuttering type then practice your spiels. Think first and then compose what you have to say in your head. And then just say it. Remember, you don't have to impress the other person.

4. *Use "I" statements*

Use "I think…" or "I feel…" more often. Don't use the accusatory "you think…" or "you felt…" line that your narcissist used on you. It's not who you are, remember.

5. *Stay calm*

Being assertive doesn't mean that you have to be excited all the time. But sometimes you can feel too excited when someone talks to you and the other person actually cares. Calm yourself first and then compose your thoughts. Go through steps 1 to 4 above before you say your first word.

6. *Understand and accept differences*

All your life a narcissist has dismissed your thoughts and your views. You're not like that. When you state your opinion and another person disagrees, tell yourself that it is okay. Accept the fact that there will be others who will have a different opinion. For some people, this will take some practice depending on how much they were abused in the past.

7. Set boundaries

Believe it or not, the boundaries of proper behavior and communication that you set with your narcissist are just as applicable to other people. Why? Well, because those are your limits and your limits are yours.

Practice these habits one by one, step by step, until they become second-nature to you.

Conclusion
From Freedom to a New Life

Thank you for downloading and reading this book.

We have covered a lot of topics from the start. If you applied each principle and guideline that was mentioned here, you would have taken the first steps in your recovery.

Yes, they are just your first steps.

If there is one truth that you should know at this point, it is the fact that recovering from narcissistic abuse will be anything but smooth. In fact, it will usually feel like a roller coaster of sorts.

There will be times when the past will haunt you. There will be times when you will feel like there is something missing in your life. There will be times when all you want to do is breakdown and cry.

Let it out—let all the pain out and watch it all wash away.

After going through all of the advice mentioned in this book, your next step is to find further strengthening. Join a support group and find people whom you can trust. Live your life.

You may also find that therapy sessions will help you get over your anxieties. Yoga, meditation, affirmations, sports, art, music, and getting in touch with nature may help you get that sense of self that you were looking for.

Whatever you do, know this that there is a bright future ahead. Others have succeeded and if they did so can you.

In fact, here is an outlook of what life has in store for you. As you recover from narcissistic abuse, here are a few prospects into what you can become:

- **You will become a person with a higher capacity to empathize and a heart full of compassion.** You can use this to uplift others who may still be on their way to recovery.
- **You will gain the ability to solve problems on your own and with better efficiency.** You have been through a lifetime of troubles. Learn from that experience. Learn that you have the power to solve problems.
- **You become a person of authenticity and integrity.** You have lived through lies and you have been lied to a lot. You know what it's like to be made fool of. You don't want that to happen to another person. Be a person of integrity. You are someone that others can trust.
- **The power to take responsibility and ownership.** A lot of survivors of narcissistic abuse become people of humility and integrity. They are also people who will take responsibility for any action. They are people who do not make excuses and will follow through every project.
- **The capacity to evolve and mature.** A lot of people who have been abused by narcissists have grown to maturity rather quickly. They are empathic survivors and they can adapt to different types of relationships—well they've been through the worst of it all. Now they can conquer all. If they get into a relationship they sometimes become some of the most mature and intimate people on earth.

There is a lot of hope for you as you deal with the ups and downs of dealing with a narcissist. There will be plenty of challenges along the way and it's not an easy road. With determination and the right help from others who have trodden the same road to recovery you will succeed.

To your success,

Thanks again for downloading this book.

www.ingramcontent.com/pod-product-compliance
Lightning Source LLC
Chambersburg PA
CBHW070327120526
44590CB00017B/2829